James Kemsley

The CARTOON Book

Hints on drawing cartoons, caricatures and comic strips

ASHTON SCHOLASTIC

SYDNEY AUCKLAND NEW YORK TORONTO LONDON

This book is respectfully dedicated to my colleagues in the Australian Black and White Artists' Club.

Thanks to my wife, Helen, for her skills, time, understanding and affection, without which this book may still be a year away from completion.

Kemsley, James, 1948–
  The cartoon book
  ISBN 0 86896 509 X

  1. Cartooning—Juvenile literature. 2. Caricature—Juvenile literature. I. Title.
  741.5

Text and illustrations copyright © James Kemsley 1990.

Ginger Meggs comic strip on page 40 is reproduced by permission of Jimera Pty Ltd.

First published in 1990 by Ashton Scholastic Pty Limited (Inc. in NSW), PO Box 579, Gosford 2250.

Typeset by InterType, Surry Hills, NSW.
Typeset in Helvetica medium.
Printed in Hong Kong

10 9 8 7 6 5 4 3 2   0 1 2 3 4 5 / 9

CONTENTS

ABOUT THIS BOOK...

I believe that anyone can draw cartoons. All they need are a few hints to set them on the right track, self-confidence and heaps of

PRACTICE, PRACTICE, PRACTICE!

This book will take care of my first point—hints. The other two are up to you.

At some stage during their life, most people try to draw a humorous drawing, that is, a cartoon. They quickly become discouraged when it looks nothing like the professional cartoons they see in magazines and newspapers.

The way professionals achieve that clean, confident line is by working hard at it every day of the week. In other words—practising.

This book has not been designed to prepare you for a job as the editorial cartoonist on a large metropolitan newspaper or as a famous-name cartoonist on a widely read glossy magazine, or to draw the world's widest syndicated comic strip. If it does, congratulations! What I hope will happen is that you will find out that I'm right when I say anyone can draw cartoons, in their own particular style. Maybe if nothing else you will then discover the fun of creating your own characters and funny situations, the enjoyment of designing your own greeting cards and posters and the relaxation of losing yourself in a world of ink and paper.

What to use

Your nearest art shop will no doubt be able to show you a vast range of art paper and an even vaster range of pens and nibs: dip pens, refillable pens, pens with convenient little plastic ink cartridges, fountain pens, mapping pens, even disposable pens. Some are fairly cheap, others are very, very expensive.

You could try using paper and pens like these:

And . .

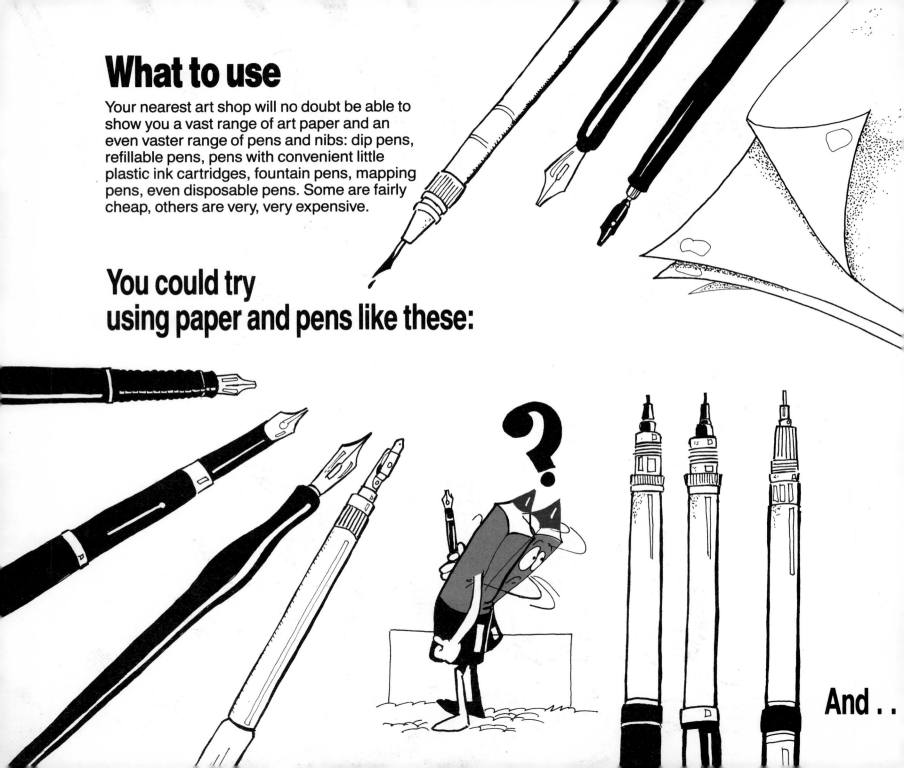

. . . inks and brushes like these:

rich black inks, inks in every colour of the rainbow and lots more; round brushes, square brushes, thin brushes, fat brushes, flat brushes, even toothbrushes!

DRAWING INK

MORE INK

STILL MORE INK

EVEN ANOTHER INK

And . . .

. . . you could try these pencils and erasers:

wax pencils, carbon pencils, charcoal pencils, retractable pencils and an eraser for all of them and for ink as well.

Once you've mastered black and white you can start experimenting with coloured pencils and inks.

And then . . .

. . . felt- and fibre-tipped pens and markers.

These come in all sizes and shapes and are easy and convenient to use.

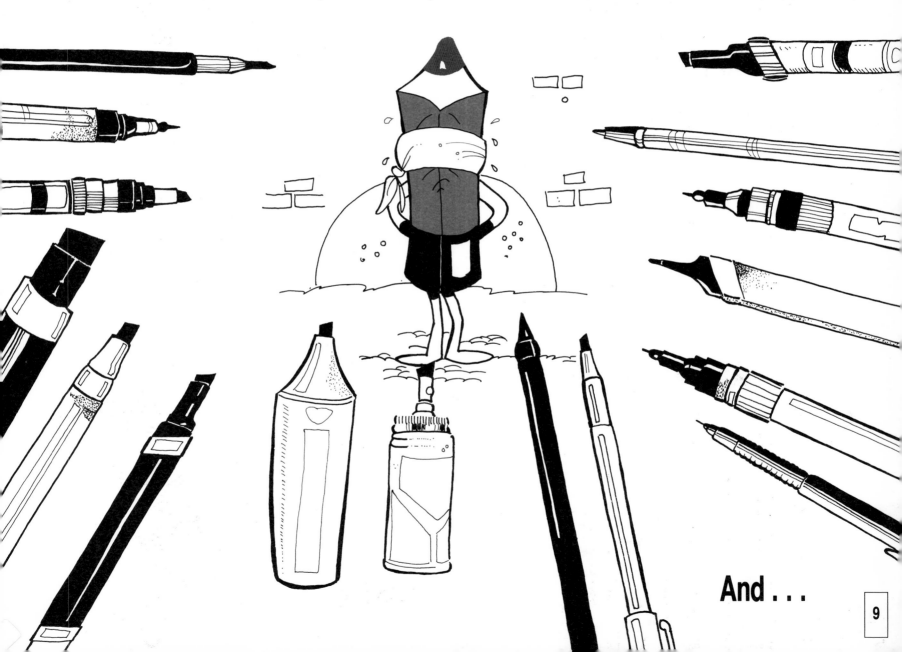

And . . .

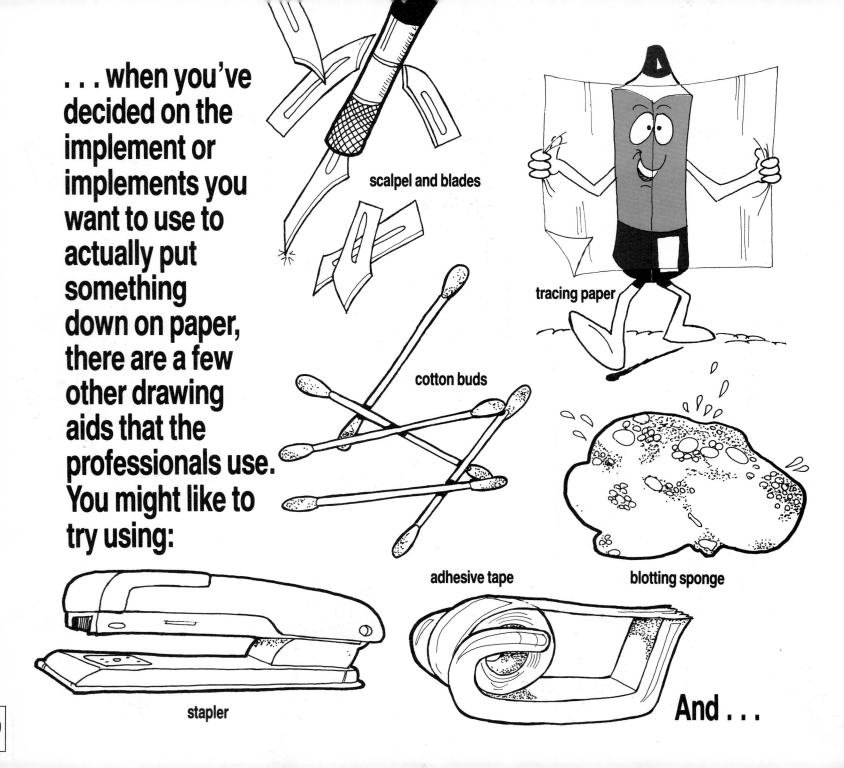

. . . when you've decided on the implement or implements you want to use to actually put something down on paper, there are a few other drawing aids that the professionals use. You might like to try using:

scalpel and blades

tracing paper

cotton buds

blotting sponge

adhesive tape

stapler

And . . .

10

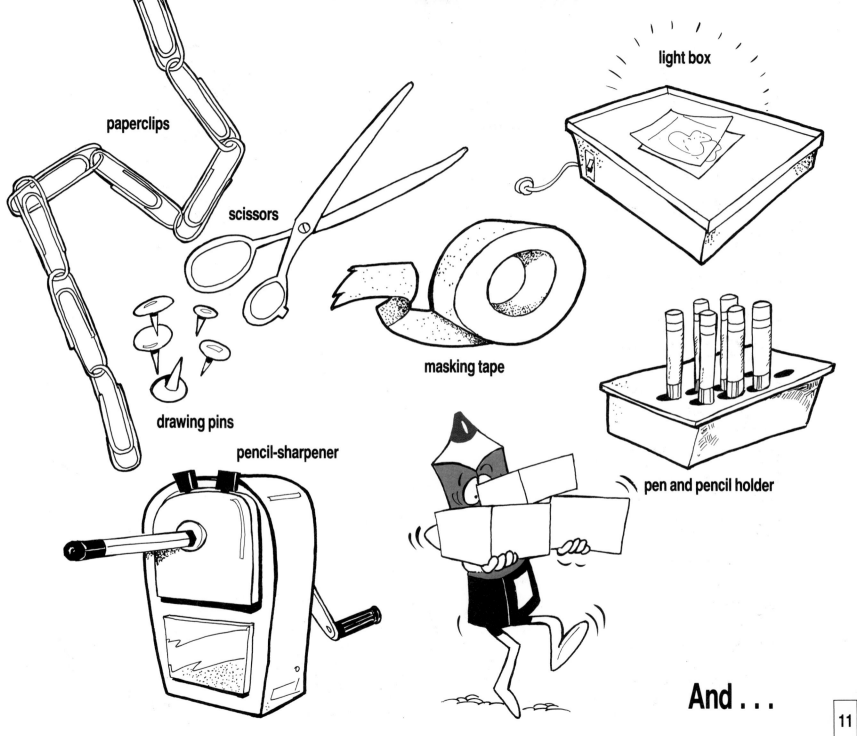

paperclips

scissors

drawing pins

pencil-sharpener

masking tape

light box

pen and pencil holder

And . . .

11

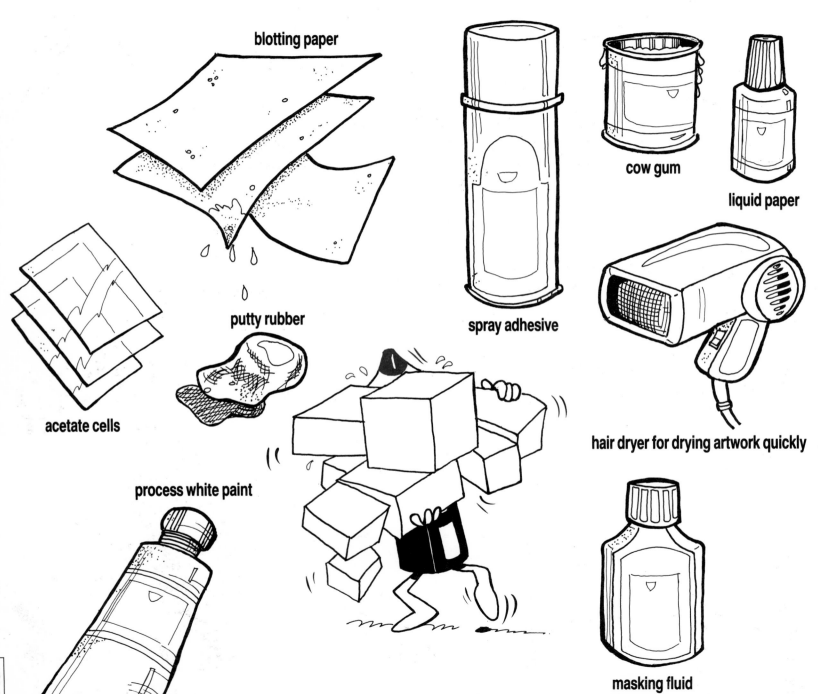

blotting paper

cow gum

liquid paper

putty rubber

spray adhesive

hair dryer for drying artwork quickly

acetate cells

process white paint

masking fluid

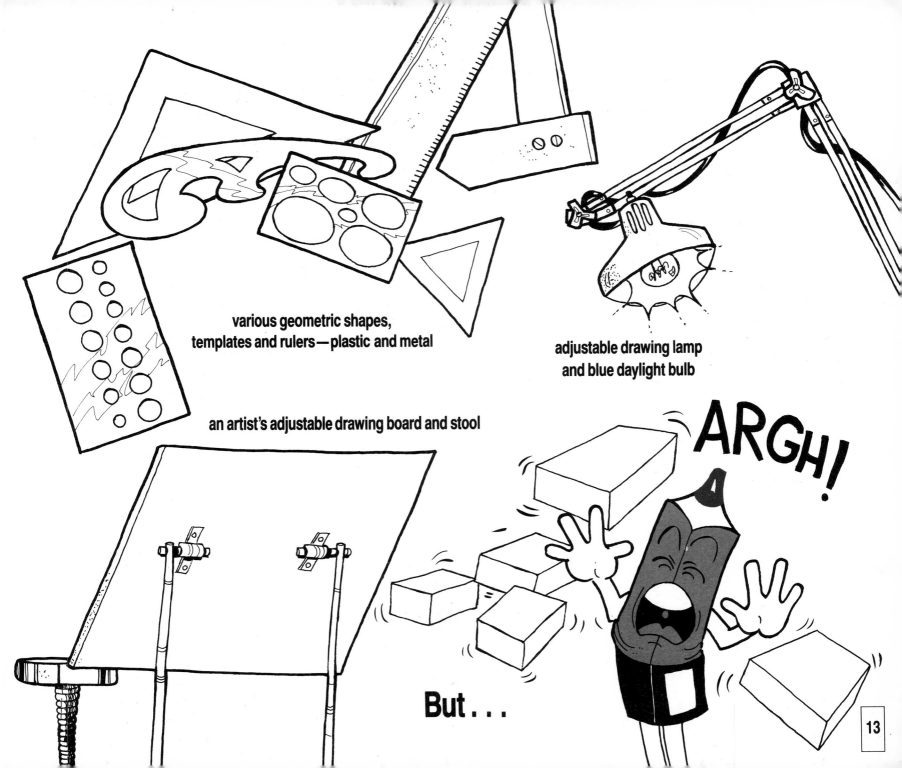

various geometric shapes,
templates and rulers—plastic and metal

adjustable drawing lamp
and blue daylight bulb

an artist's adjustable drawing board and stool

ARGH!

But . . . .

... at this stage of your cartooning career you really only need two things to get you going:

a pencil,

preferably a soft one, and

a piece of blank paper.

The unused side of used computer paper or the type of paper butchers use to wrap meat will be perfect—without the meat!

Another three things could come in handy: an eraser—a soft one if possible, a ruler—an old school one will be fine and, last of all, a pencil sharpener.

Note: professional cartoonists use or are capable of using everything described on the preceding pages (and lots more as well). Although the odd one or two are mentioned in the course of this book, their use and place in the art of cartooning are best left to more advanced books on the subject. Books that you may or may not want to delve into once you discover your hidden talent. There is a list of resources on page 64. Any reader seriously considering a professional cartooning career should make sure they learn the use of each and every implement I've listed.

**Now you know what you need,
here are some**

To begin . . .

Cartoons, caricatures and comic strips all have one thing in common,

expression.

So that's where we'll start.

Simple dots can say
heaps in cartoons.
Like this . . . . they are just dots.

But add a line or two and they can be:

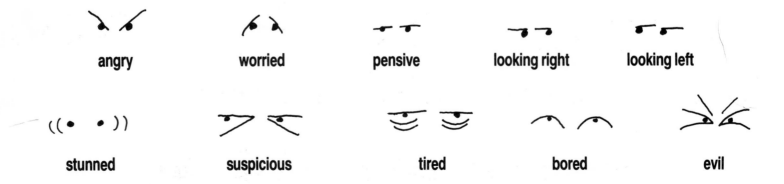

| angry | worried | pensive | looking right | looking left |

| stunned | suspicious | tired | bored | evil |

See how many more variations you can come up with.

The dot can also say a lot when popped inside a circle,
or an egg shape.

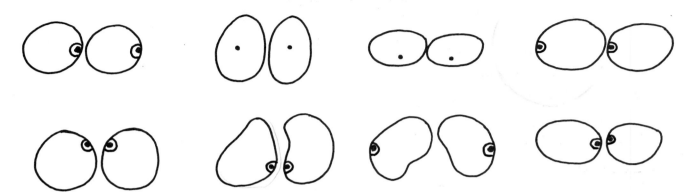

Then when you add the lines we used before:

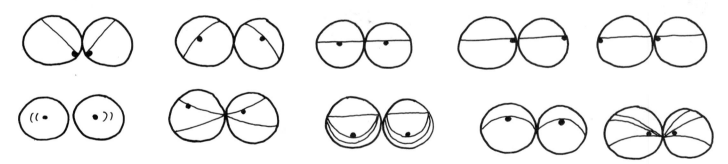

They become very talkative, don't they?

Now you know the basics of cartoon expression
you can use them on . . .

heads – these can be any shape or size you want them to be.

We'll take a couple of those weird shapes . . .

. . . and add the dots

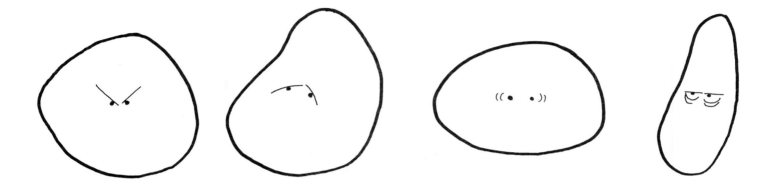

and the circles.

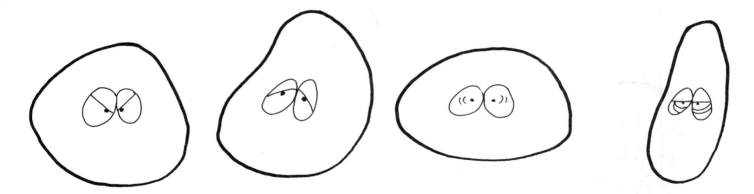

You can see we have the base
for some fun faces.

The **mouth** is equally as important to a character's expression as the eyes.

The mood of a character and therefore the eyes usually determine the type of mouth that should go with them.

By matching unlikely pairs you can end up with a character in quite a different mood. Take our angry sketch as an example.

  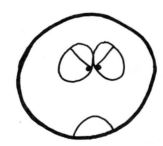 

Experiment with various combinations and see what you can invent.

Noses, eyes, eyebrows and hair

come in an endless variety and are easy to add.

By using the original shape but putting the features to left or right we get a side-on view, a profile, of the character.

As they do in reality, cartoon **bodies** also come in all shapes and sizes.

Once you've decided on the one you like pop on the head, with or without neck, it doesn't matter!

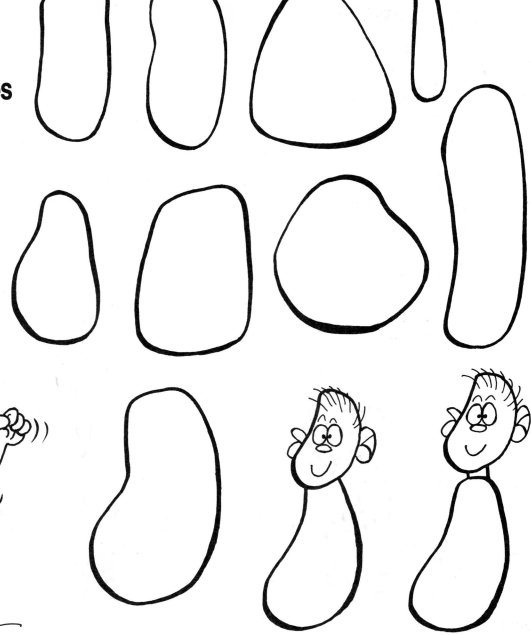

Where you put your character's **arms and legs** depends on whether you want it . . .

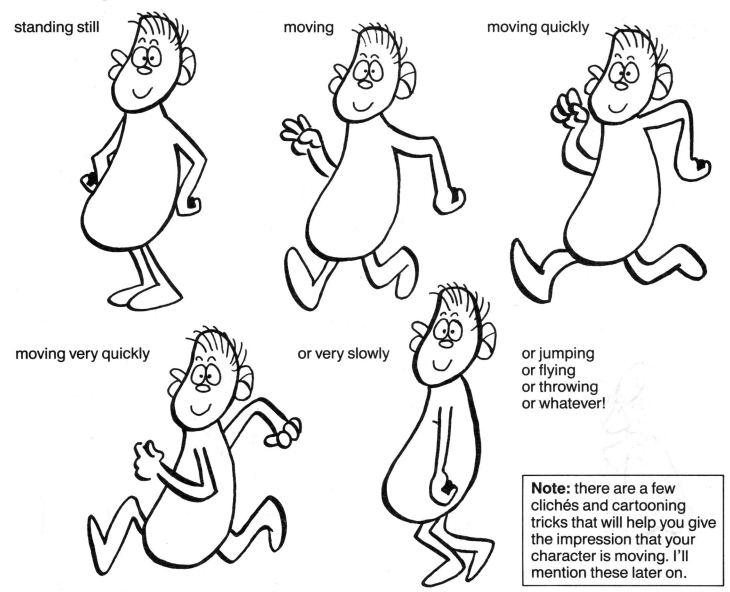

standing still

moving

moving quickly

moving very quickly

or very slowly

or jumping
or flying
or throwing
or whatever!

Note: there are a few clichés and cartooning tricks that will help you give the impression that your character is moving. I'll mention these later on.

When it comes to **finishing or dressing up** your character the choices are unlimited.

Your original cartoon character should be able to be adapted to any age, sex or costume with the minimum of fuss.

Hands are a very important part of a cartoon character.

Wherever possible they should add to the action of the drawing, rather than hang limply down the side of the character's body. There are times you may want that feeling from a cartoon, but generally 'doing' hands are better than 'dead' hands.

The types of hands cartoonists draw can range from being almost lifelike to squiggles on the end of an arm. Some cartoonists and most animators find a character looks better and is easier to draw with only three fingers and a thumb. All can be equally effective if used in the right circumstances.

Drawing nails and hand creases can clutter up a cartoon, but don't let that stop you if you like the effect.

Note: if you have trouble with hands, you can always put them in the character's pockets or behind its back until you're confident in drawing them. Flick over to page 35 and you'll see what I mean.

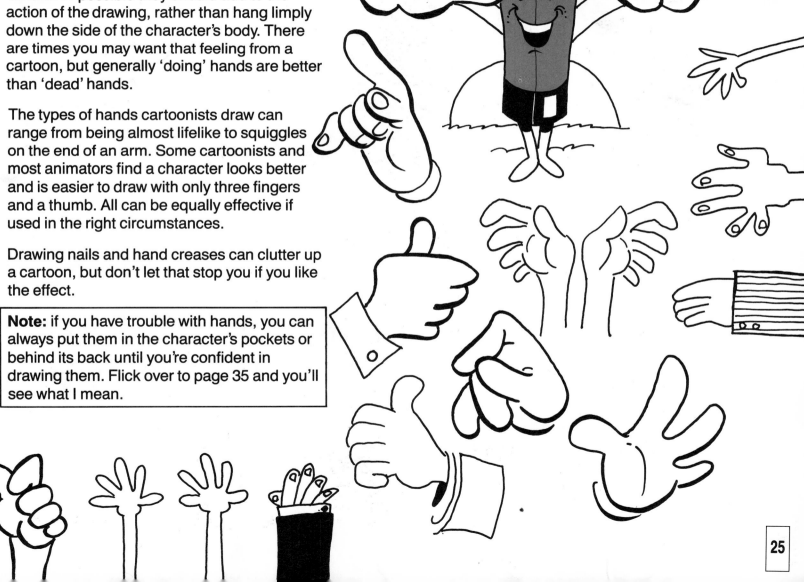

Feet and shoes

As with hands, almost anything goes. Draw the type you feel comfortable with and try and make them more than something dangling off, or stuck on to, your character's ankles.

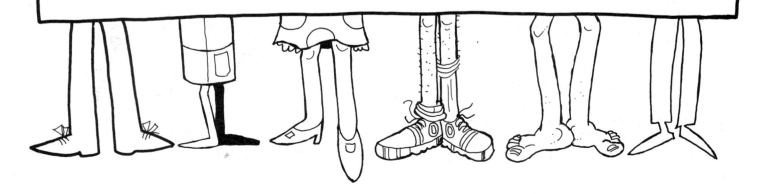

STYLE

We pause from actually putting pencil on paper for a moment to talk about style. The way **you** draw. (Anyway, your pencil should need sharpening!)

If you have been cartooning whilst reading this book, you will have already noticed you have a certain style, that is a way of drawing, an individual appearance to your work. Like handwriting, a drawing style is unique to each person.

Although you might like to study and copy the work of other cartoonists (virtually every cartoonist started trying to draw like the artist they most admired), ultimately your own personal style will emerge. It will be the way you feel most comfortable when drawing. Just as trying to copy someone's handwriting each time you write would be a drag, the same can be said about continually trying to draw like someone else.

Your style might be smooth and sophisticated, childlike and innocent, sketchy and rough. Whatever it is, it is you and it is the style that you should continue to refine and develop. Only that way will you achieve the confidence of line and individuality of the great cartoonists.

Animals

It's often said some people prefer the company of animals to humans, many cartoonists do, at least they prefer drawing them. Apart from the obvious changes in their appearance, all the cartooning hints I've given so far apply to animals as well.

Play around with shapes.

Add circles and dots,

the nose, ears and mouth

and a funny body and legs.

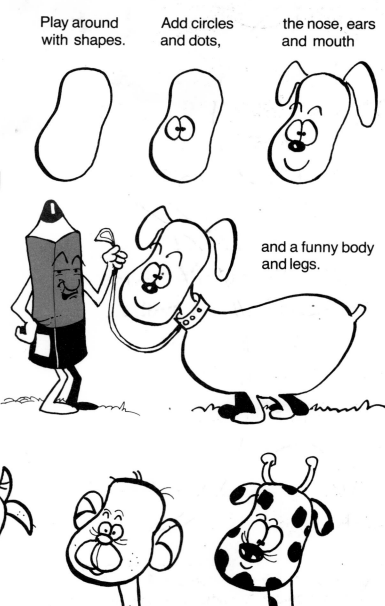

Often the same funny shape can be adapted to various animals.

Humanimals

Don't try and find the above word in a dictionary, it doesn't exist. Not as far as I'm aware, anyway. I use it to describe the cartoonist's way of giving animals human features, as opposed to page 28 where animals act like some humans but still look like animals. Team logos are a good example of animal heads on human bodies.

Once you get started on these you won't be able to stop.

Note: the correct word for the above is anthropomorphism. Not only does it apply to animals but to fruit, plants and inanimate objects as well.

Fruit and plants

These are simple to draw and make interesting cartoons, especially on greeting cards, letterheads, flyers and posters. By applying the earlier hints you can create an endless supply of amusing, fun-looking characters.

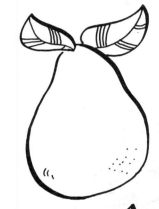

Cartoonists' clichés

Almost an official set of clichés has developed over the years to help cartoonists convey specific ideas to their readers. There is nothing unoriginal or wrong in using them, in fact there may even be occasions where not using them is a mistake. You can be assured of immediate reader communication with clichés.

Here is a selection—but I'm sure you can come up with lots more.

Commas around a character show it's moving and a squiggle or shadowy shape beneath it tells us it is in midair.

A light bulb tells your readers the character has had a bright idea.

Stars and planets indicate a crash, collision or punch.

To make a character run, add a squiggle below it and it becomes airborne; cloud-like shapes behind give it a wake; the smaller rectangles are paper caught in the wake; droplets show the character perspiring, and shading in the cheek area gives the impression that the character is hot from running. Finally, streaky lines trailing behind give it speed.

The double take turns the character quickly.

Droplets around the eyes can also tell us the character is crying—the more drops the more intense the crying.

Putting eyeballs or pupils outside their sockets means the character has been startled or is terrified.

Stars, rings and various sized circles are the clichés for being dazed or stunned. Note the position of the character's eyeballs. Cross-eyed is another good cliché.

'S' lines show the character has been zig-zagging.

With or without a saw cutting through a log, Z Z Z Z is the universal sign for sleeping and snoring.

Sparks and puffs of dust give the impression of stopping suddenly.

Hearts show a character in love or smitten.

There are many, many cartoon clichés and it is a good idea to keep in a file, examples of those you like or want to use.

Less is more? More or less!

Some artists will argue that cartoons should be simple and uncomplicated with a minimum of line work and background and that a good, crisp clean drawing is the way to go. On the other hand, there are hundreds of successful cartoonists and comic-strip artists who fill every available dot of space they are given. The choice is personal. There are no hard and fast rules.

Below are two examples of the same illustration. The one that appeals most to you is probably the style you will choose to follow. However, there is no reason to be locked into one or the other. It will all depend on the drawing you are doing at the time and the style that most suits it.

If it feels good, draw it!

A sneaky hint . . .

Hide it until you can draw it.

Chances are when you begin to draw cartoons, there will be elements which will worry you. Something that you find hard to capture on paper the way you see it in your head. This can cause the lack of a confident line in your entire piece of work.

If you follow my number one hint and practise, practise, practise, eventually the problems will cease to exist, but until then you might find it easier to draw around or hide the problems.

Hands and feet seem to be a common worry. As I said earlier, if necessary, hands can be put in pockets.

Here's another couple of sneakies:

Two characters behind a fence—no need to worry about the feet.

Behind a rubbish bin or rock— again, no feet.

Arms behind the back— again, no hands.

Carrying something—no hands.

I'm sure you can work out a lot more.

HINTS ON LETTERING YOUR WORK

USUALLY CARTOON CAPTIONS ARE TYPESET, WHILE COMIC-STRIP DIALOGUE IS HAND LETTERED. THERE ARE, OF COURSE, LOTS OF EXAMPLES OF BOTH TO THE CONTRARY. AGAIN IT BRINGS US BACK TO STYLE. SOME LETTERING IS HURRIED AND SCRATCHY, SOME IS STRAIGHT AND DELIBERATE. AS WITH THE DRAWING, IT DEPENDS ON YOU AND THE FEEL YOU WANT YOUR WORK TO CONVEY TO ITS READERS. IN SOME COUNTRIES CARTOONISTS OPT TO EMPLOY FULL-TIME LETTERERS TO LETTER FOR THEM. YOU WON'T BE ABLE TO DO THAT, SO ...

1 Always use capital letters, they are easier to read when reduced in size.

2 To emphasise a word or words, write them in **bold.**

3 Work out how much area you will need for your lettering by writing it out roughly on a piece of scrap paper.

4 Never break a word in the middle. It looks awful and is hard to read.

HINTS ON CARICATURE... EXAGGERATION and Distortion

Of all the cartooning arts, caricature takes the most patience to develop, refine and master. It is the one that is more a natural ability than an acquired skill. Still, you'll be surprised what a lot of practice and, even more, perseverance will produce.

Exaggeration and distortion are two words that quickly come to mind when discussing caricaturing. However, caricaturing is not simply a case of drawing big noses and weird ears, or little bodies and smaller people. It's carefully studying a person to capture not only a lampooned likeness, but their personality as well.

Don't be confused by the word exaggeration, it doesn't necessarily mean big and broad. In a lot of cases it might well be that certain features are drawn smaller or narrower.

Where there is something distinctive about the way a subject speaks or moves their face, walks, sits or stands, try and incorporate that into the caricature as well.

Some caricaturists draw from life, others use photographs. Many use a combination of the two. Here's an example of a caricature from a photo.

Features that may be outstanding:

HAIR

NOSE

TEETH

GLASSES

MOUSTACHE

SHAPE OF HEAD

CLOTHING MAY ALSO BE ADAPTABLE

KEMSLEY

Note: not so much a note as a bit of friendly advice—try to avoid caricaturing friends and relations. Things are never quite the same when they know how you see them!

on drawing a

There are three types of comic strip.

1 The large, multi-panel comic known as the Sunday strip.

This type of strip can be anywhere from between eight to twelve panels long. Sometimes it can be a complete story with a beginning, a middle and an end. Other times it might be a serial that is continued from week to week.

2 The Sunday strip's smaller brother, the daily.

This type of strip can be two, three or four panels long. Sometimes it can even be a single panel. Like the Sunday strip it can also be a complete story or a serial. Normally the joke is set up in the first panel, built upon in the middle panel and the ending, usually called the tag, comes in the final panel.

3 The comic book.

This strip, as the name implies, is in book form. Normally it consists of one long story or a series of short stories over a number of pages.

Despite their different sizes, all follow the same basic rules.

Who do you want to read your comic strip?

Different comics have different readers—very few comics appeal to everyone. Therefore it's important to know your audience. For example, it could be aimed at:

 **kids**

 **adults**

 **oldies**

 who are either **up-market**

 or **down-market**

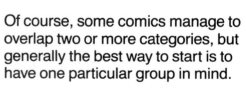

Of course, some comics manage to overlap two or more categories, but generally the best way to start is to have one particular group in mind.

Just as your readership determines your type of humour, and to a certain extent your style of drawing, your type of humour and style of drawing can equally determine your readership.

Don't be too confused, you will quickly learn who are reading or are not reading your comic.

Once you have decided on the readership you hope to attract, you can then decide on the type of **characters** that will attract them!

Your characters can be anyone or anything, that's the fun part of drawing a comic. Reality needn't be any part of it.

Your characters are probably alive and well and already running around in your imagination.

All you have to do is to pop them out onto your page through your pencil.

There is no limit to the types of characters you can bring to life in comic strips.

They can be:

people

animals

insects

plants

rocks

FAR OUT!

EVEN A PENCIL!

or just about anything!

When it comes to designing the **look** of your comic-strip characters, follow the simple hints I've given you throughout this book.

After all, a comic strip is only a sequence of single cartoons strung together.

But! When it comes to designing their **personalities**

remember no matter how short or how long, how funny or how serious your comic strip is going to be it is, after all, a story. The best stories have many different types of characters, some the readers like, others they dislike. In short, goodies and baddies.

Types

Try not to have characters too similar in either personality or look. Readers will soon find the lack of variety very dull and stop reading your strip.

You will find after you've been drawing them for a while your cast will begin to develop physically. There's more than a good chance that they will bear little resemblance to the characters you started out with. If you've given them a strong three-dimensional personality and good stories, your readers probably won't even be aware of the changes.

Don't worry that the look of your comic strip changes, it shows you are developing as a cartoonist and becoming more confident with the things you draw.

Find some very old copies of your favourite strip and you will see what I mean when I talk about changes.

Work out your cast then you will be ready to create a strip.

Humour

This section focuses on hints on the technicalities of putting comic strips together, rather than teaching you how to be funny or how to write comic strips.

However, having said that, I gladly pass on a piece of advice given to me when I first dreamed of drawing a comic strip:

Think of something funny, then work backwards.

In other words, know where your story is going. Know your tag first, then construct your lead up. You'll find that is the easiest way to work, either on a 'daily', 'Sunday' or even a comic book. Once you've worked out the last panel you'll know exactly what's needed to fill in the rest.

As an example, let's take a joke.

FIRST PERSON: I hear your dad ran his old car into a lightpole?
SECOND PERSON: Yeah.
FIRST PERSON: Is he okay?
SECOND PERSON: I'll say he is. He did $300 worth of improvements.

Take a piece of scrap paper and scribble out three panels, put the tag in the last one.

That leaves us two panels in which to find a home for the rest of the joke.

Easy! The same rules apply for 'Sundays' and comic books.

Plotting your stories

Always work out your stories on scrap paper long before you put them on a bright new, and possibly expensive, piece of art board.

Not only should you use a bit of rough paper to plot in your dialogue, but you can work out the placement, shape and composition of your pictures at the same time.

The *Ginger Meggs* strip on page 40 would have begun looking something like this:

It's showtime!

If you looked closely at the *Ginger Meggs* rough on page 48 you will have noticed I used various cinema terminology. Words such as 'two shot' and 'close-up'. That's because I believe every strip I draw is a little movie and I'm the director.

TWO BEE

Just as a movie would be dull and boring if it was all filmed as a wide shot, so would a comic strip.

There was a time when film-makers and comic-strip artists used to do everything on a wide shot, but after experimenting they found the public liked a variety of shots and angles.

You may not have thought about it before, but the combinations of two shots, reverses, close-ups, crowd shots and so on may be the reason you have either liked or disliked a particular comic strip or movie. Next time you're in the cinema, take note of the technique of the director and see if you can translate his movie-making ideas to your comic strip.

Shapes

Apart from the type of comic strip you decide to draw, another important factor to consider is the size and shape of the strip.

If you want to sell it, a comic strip must conform to the standard width and length of the newspapers and magazines in which you might like to see it appear.

A quick measure with a ruler is the easiest way to check on sizes. Providing the outer size and shape conform, your panels within the comic can vary in size and shape if that's the feel you want.

So, before you send examples of your handiwork to an editor, make sure it is going to fit snugly into their publication.

Once you've decided on the characters, the story, the shape and the size, you're ready to start drawing—almost!

Very few, if any, artists draw to size, by that I mean few draw their cartoons or comic strips the size that they appear when they are published.

It is much easier to draw them a size that you feel comfortable with, then have them reduced to the size required.

You will find you can get a clean, crisper line that way and your eyes and hand won't give out on you midway through the cartoon.

But how can you be sure that when your drawing is reduced it will be the shape and size you want it to be? Here's how:

Start by lightly drawing the shape and size you want in the bottom left-hand corner of your page.

Next, run a diagonal line from corner to corner extending it to the area in which you want to draw.

Extend the left-hand side line and the base line of your original box. The point where the horizontal and vertical lines meet with the diagonal line will form an exact enlargement of that original box.

POINT WHERE ALL THREE LINES MEET

SIZE OF ORIGINAL DRAWING

SIZE OF PUBLISHED CARTOON

Note: remember that not only the size of your lines are reduced but their thickness is as well.

Panel by panel

The type of panel in which your characters appear and the story unfolds is very important. It sets the feel of the comic strip before a word is read.

You will know the image you want your comic strip to have and should draw your panels accordingly.

Here are some different styles:

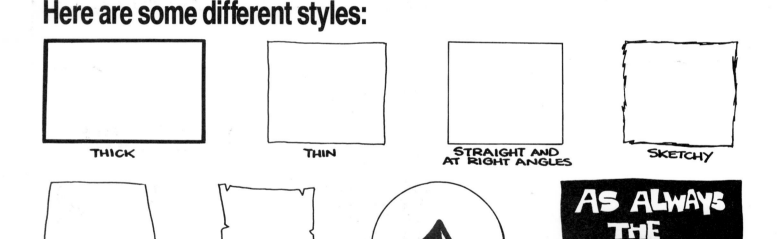

THICK

THIN

STRAIGHT AND AT RIGHT ANGLES

SKETCHY

NOTHING LIKE RIGHT ANGLES

HAVE BITS MISSING

SOMETIMES ROUND

AS ALWAYS THE CHOICE IS YOURS.

Sometimes there is no need for a panel at all. This can create an interesting effect. You can see how I've done that in both the 'Sunday' and 'daily' on pages 40 and 41.

Whatever style of panel you decide on, you should keep the entire strip in that style. Mixing up panels only creates a messy visual effect. However, different shapes and sizes in the same style can create an interesting effect.

Comic-strip characters communicate with each other through
speech balloons.

Like the panels, these can take many shapes.

... THEY COULD HAVE ROUND CORNERS...

... OR THEY COULD BE OVAL SHAPED...

... OR RECTANGULAR...

... THEY MIGHT EVEN BE CLOUD-LIKE...

... OR RUN FROM ONE SIDE OF THE PANEL TO THE OTHER...

...AND SOMETIMES HAVE NO SHAPE AT ALL!

Unlike the panels, mixing up balloons within a strip
can create an interesting effect.

There are also lots of
cliché speech balloons

that not only tell who is speaking, but also show the type of mood the character is in. Some of these are:

I'M FREEZING, EITHER THAT OR I'M GIVING SOMEONE THE COLD SHOULDER.

I'M THINKING.

I'M WHISPERING.

I'M DEPRESSED OR GLOOMY.

I'M MAD AND I'M SHOUTING LOUDLY.

I'M SCARED.

I'M SINGING MY WORDS.

Normally you would not use any of these in every panel of a comic strip, but rather once or twice to get a message across to the reader.

Just as special speech balloons set the mood of a comic strip, so does **special lettering.**

Here are just a few ways to use lettering to make your comic strip more interesting:

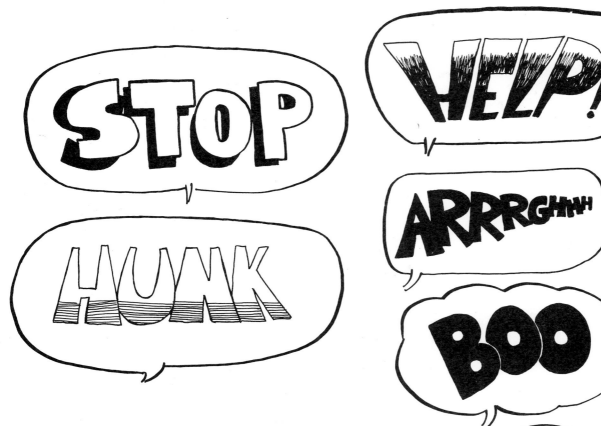

The speech balloon hint applies to special lettering too: it is a way to make a point in a panel or two and not something to be used in every panel. Unless, of course, there is a specific visual effect you want to achieve.

Special lettering is also a major part of another comic strip cliché—the use of onomatopoeia.

Onomatopoeia

This refers to words that are spelt the way they sound. A very important tool in a comic-strip artist's bag of tricks.

These words help break up the look of a page as well as giving it a feeling of movement, action and excitement. Especially if they are also drawn the way they sound.

There are thousands of sound words you can use and millions you can invent. That's right—invent! A comic strip is one of the few places where you can put words into the language and have them immediately accepted by readers.

Hints on signing your Signature

The last thing you do before you can say a piece of artwork is complete, is to sign it. That way your readers know who to admire (or blame!).

The signature you finish off a cartoon or comic strip with should not be the same one you use to sign letters or other documents. As much thought should go into working out what will eventually be your trademark as goes into your drawing. It should be something crisp and clean that is easily recognisable and readable. It will say a lot about the type of cartoonist you are.

Start looking at the signature on the work of your favourite comic-strip artist or cartoonist. You will see it is distinctive and unique to that person.

Many of the great artists are known as much by the way they sign a piece of work as they are for their style.

Hints on

DEALING with MiSTAKS

We all make them, some more than others, but that's no reason to panic.

With mistakes, our first tendency is to screw up the offending drawing and practise our favourite basketball shot into the nearest wastepaper bin. That's okay if you've only roughed something out or just started your assignment. But what if you were only strokes away from finishing that long awaited masterpiece or half a panel off your best-ever comic strip? Or using that super-expensive piece of art board? Or have only one piece of art board left on which to finish an important job?

There are alternatives to tomorrow's rubbish collection . . .

. . . if you've only been drawing in pencil the solution is easy— **use an eraser!**

Removing ink mistakes or ink accidents is a little more complicated.

Imagine you're using a pen that decides to blob all over the place or a top flies off an ink bottle that was supposed to be screwed on tightly.

1 Quickly and carefully sop it up with tissue or blotting paper. Use the edges rather than plopping it flat down on the blob, that will only spread the ink all over your drawing. When the blob is almost sopped up then you can use the flat surface.

2 Using a clean brush and clean water, brush over the remains of the ink until it has disappeared as much as you think it will. Don't use great splashes of water. Small amounts applied often will make sure you know when to stop before the paper is saturated and ruined.

3 Paint over the area with process white paint. Again, use a little at a time; by building it up gradually in a series of thin coats, rather than slapping a hunk down, it will be easier to draw over.

How to get rid of an unwanted line or three.

As with blobs, you can paint them out or, if you have been using very thick paper or board, you can scrape away your mistake or little accidents with a scalpel or razor blade.

Use only new, sharp blades and take extreme care not to scrape a hole through your paper and not to cut off a finger or two. Blood and bone are hard to remove from artwork!

If the mistake is **really** bad—

the whole panel of a strip for instance—the easiest and quickest thing to do is simply to redraw that one panel, then paste it over the disaster area. Use a dry glue that won't soak through the paper (making it transparent and thereby revealing the original drawing). Done the right way, the paste over will go unnoticed when the comic is reproduced.

Many artists even redraw and paste down individual characters in a cartoon they are not happy with.

Of course, if you think the mistake is **really, really, really bad news** – then there's the wastepaper bin!

Hints on research

Keep a

MORGUE

that is, a scrap collection of everything!

No, cartoonists don't keep dead bodies, none that I'm aware of anyway. As far as a cartoonist is concerned, a morgue is their reference library. Something they can't do without. From today onwards start a file of photographs, illustrations, cartoons, and newspaper and magazine clippings of just about everything: people, places, birds, cars, insects, fashion, flags, houses, rocks, bridges, trees, trampolines, ships, clouds, empty drink cans, machines, motorbikes, tombstones, animals and maps.

Yes, anything and everything!

Some lucky people can draw almost anything from memory or imagination. The rest of us aren't so lucky. But once you've set up a complete morgue, your worries are over.

Finally!

I can only end with the same words I used at the start of this book:

PRACTISE
PRACTISE
PRACTISE

Good luck,

James Kemsley

Resources

A selection of other books on cartooning you might find helpful.

Harris, Rolf. *Your Cartoon Time.* Hodder & Stoughton.

Hoff, Syd. *How To Draw Cartoons.* Scholastic.

Maddocks, Peter. *How To Be A Super Cartoonist.* Elm Tree.

Maddocks, Peter. *So You Want To Be A Cartoonist?* Unwin.

McKenzie, Alan. *How To Draw and Sell . . . Comic Strips.* McDonald Orbis.

Nelson, Roy Paul. *The Art Of Cartooning.* Fell.

Reading, Bryan. *Drawing Cartoons and Caricatures.* Fontana.

Rigby, Paul. *Cartooning and Drawing Techniques.* 12 Star Product Group.

Stoner, Charles. *Pen Tips On Cartooning.* Hunt Manufacturing.

Thompson, Ross and Hewson, Bill. *How To Draw and Sell Cartoons.* Methuen.

Meglin, Nick. *The Art Of Humorous Illustration.* Watson-Guptill.

Tips From Top Cartoonists. Donnar Publications.